Historical Atlases of South Asia,
Central Asia, and the Middle East™

A HISTORICAL ATLAS OF

KYRGYZSTAN

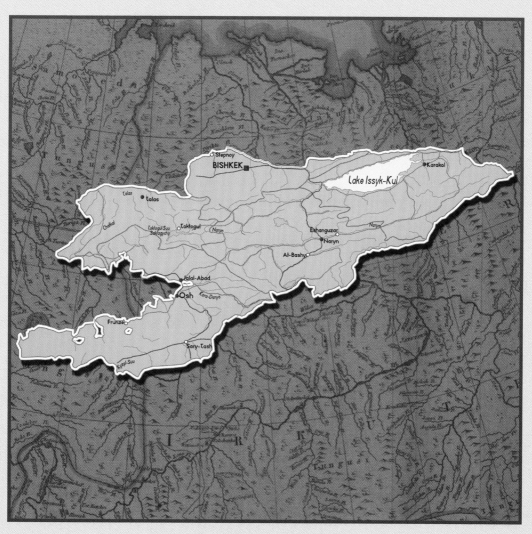

Aisha Khan

The Rosen Publishing Group, Inc., New York

To the memory of my grandfather Azim Ansari, my uncle Aftab Ahmad,
and my father-in-law, Altaf Ahmed

Published in 2004 by The Rosen Publishing Group, Inc.
29 East 21st Street, New York, NY 10010

First Edition

Library of Congress Cataloging-in-Publication Data

Khan, Aisha.
A historical atlas of Kyrgyzstan / Aisha Khan.—1st ed.
    p. cm. —(Historical atlases of South Asia, Central Asia, and the Middle East)
Summary: Maps and text chronicle the history of the former Soviet republic of Kyrgyzstan, one of the five countries of central Asia.
Includes bibliographical references (p.) and index.
Contents: Early history—The Kyrgyz arrive—The coming of the Mongols—Enter the Russians—Kirghiz Soviet Socialist Republic—Independence.
ISBN 0-8239-4499-9
1. Kyrgyzstan—History—Maps for children. 2. Kyrgyzstan—Maps for children.
[1. Kyrgyzstan—History. 2. Atlases.]
I. Title. II. Series.
G2168.71.S1K4 2004
911'.5843—dc22

2003055020

Manufactured in the United States of America

On the cover: A Kyrgyz hunter with a trained falcon *(top left)* appears next to an early Kyrgyz stele featuring a warrior *(top right)*, the current president of Kyrgystan, Askar Akayev, and a contemporary map of Kyrgystan. The background map, created by Johann Treskot, depicts the Russian Empire in 1776.

Contents

Lake Issyk-Kul

●Karakol

Terskey Ala-Too

Tien Shan

CHINA

INTRODUCTION

Kyrgyzstan (KUR-gih-stan) is one of the five countries that make up the region known as Central Asia. The other four are Kazakhstan, Turkmenistan, Uzbekistan, and Tajikistan. These five nations are bound geographically and share a common history and culture. "Kyrgyzstan" means land of the Kyrgyz, just as "Uzbekistan" means land of the Uzbeks.

In reality, however, none of these countries is home only to the people it is named after. In fact, the populations of these countries are multicultural, multilingual, and multiethnic. There are Tajiks in Kyrgyzstan, Kyrgyz in Uzbekistan, and so on. There are also Russians, Germans, and even Koreans in these countries, as well as people of various religions and languages. One of the main reasons that these countries have

This contemporary map illustrates the mountainous landlocked central Asian nation of Kyrgyzstan and the countries that surround it including Kazakhstan, China, Tajikstan, and Uzbekistan. Kyrgyzstan is a small, impoverished nation that became independent after the fall of the Soviet Union in 1991. The Kyrgyz are primarily nomadic farmers and shepherds with strong tribal traditions. Although most Kyrgyz are Muslims, about 25 percent of the country's population is Russian Orthodox.

such a mixed population is because the present borders of Central Asia were first drawn by the Union of Soviet Socialist Republics (USSR), of which present-day Russia was a part. The USSR created these Soviet republics to strengthen its own hold over them through the policy of divide and rule. The USSR also encouraged people to migrate between the republics, sending Russians into Central Asia so that there would be fewer concentrations of ethnic groups.

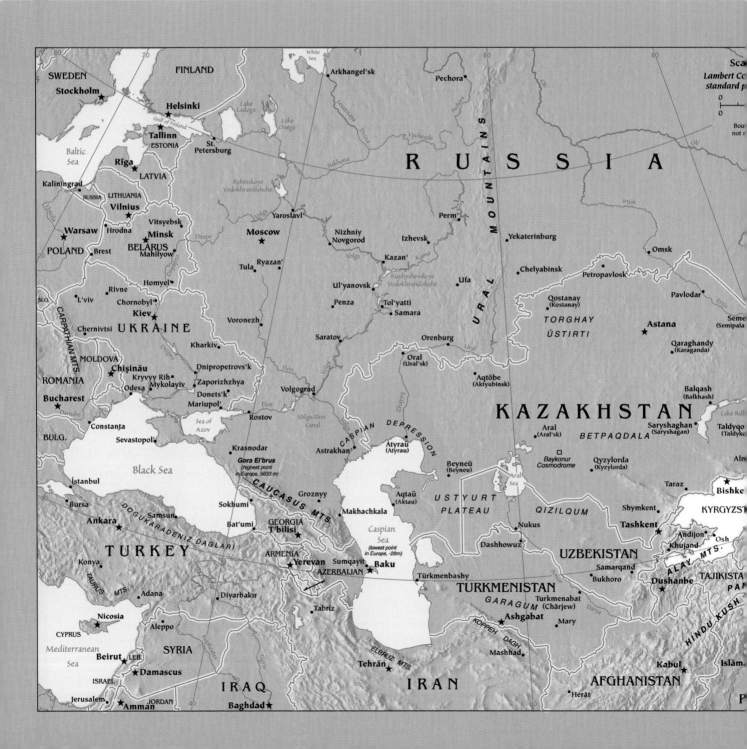

After little more than seventy years, the Soviet Union's policies failed and the country broke apart in 1991. All the Soviet republics declared themselves independent, including the five republics in Central Asia. Those republics became free to govern themselves without the Soviet government. They could hold their own elections and decide their own policies.

During the Soviet era, a veil of secrecy covered Central Asia and the rest of the Soviet Union. This was partly due to the Cold War between the United States and the USSR. The Soviet Union was very secretive. Its leaders were afraid that Western countries would try to obtain information in order to overthrow the Communist government.

With the collapse of the Soviet Union in 1991 and recent developments in the region, Western governments want to form alliances with countries there. This is partly because of the region's strategic location and its closeness to Russia, China, Europe, Iran, and Afghanistan. For example, recent efforts of diplomacy by the United States have resulted in a military alliance with Uzbekistan. This relationship allowed the United States to station U.S. troops there, which proved useful in the war on Iraq in 2003. The United States also wants to explore opportunities for business ventures in the region, since it has rich resources of natural gas, petroleum, coal, and minerals such as gold, uranium, copper, and silver.

Although Kyrgyzstan is lesser known than other Central Asian nations because of its small size, it is strategically located next to China. Kyrgyzstan also shares borders with Kazakhstan, Uzbekistan, and Tajikistan. It is a landlocked country with a population of more than 4.8 million.

The nomadic Kyrgyz first came to the north of their present home in the Chu Valley around AD 600. They slowly moved farther south of the mountain ranges of the Tien Shan. Before that, the Kyrgyz are believed to have lived in the region that is now Russia and Kazakhstan. Ethnically speaking, the Kyrgyz are

The geographical position and relative small size of Kyrgyzstan compared to other central Asian nations can be seen in this map created by the United States Central Intelligence Agency (CIA) in 2000. The map features the nations in Asia that were once considered a part of the Union of Soviet Socialist Republics (USSR), including Kazakhstan, Turkmenistan, Uzbekistan, and Kyrgystan. Although all of these countries are unique, they all share interdependencies regarding transportation, energy, and water sources.

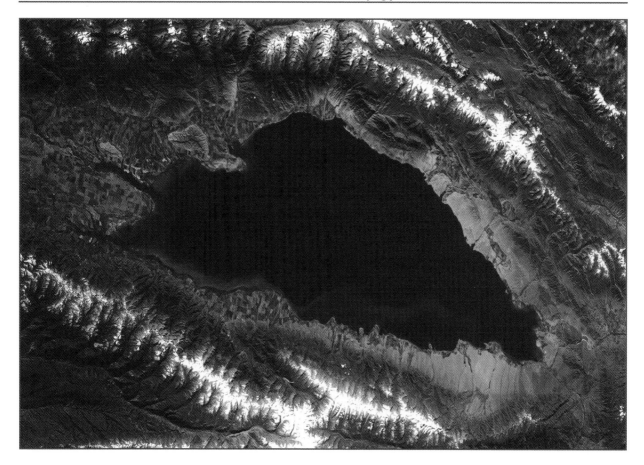

Kyrgyzstan's large mountain lake, Issyk-Kul, seen in this satellite image, is one of the country's most precious natural resources. Sometimes referred to as a "hot" lake because its high salt content keeps it from freezing over, Issyk-Kul has long been revered by the Kyrgyz, who once refused to swim in it. Bordered by the snow-capped Tien Shan mountains, the expansive 113-mile-long (182-km) lake often draws tourists to Kyrgyzstan for its picturesque beauty, though its water is not suitable for drinking or irrigation.

related to both the Mongols and the Turks. Their language, Kyrgyz, belongs to a sub-branch of the Turkish language group.

The history of Kyrgyzstan has often been obscured by other more dramatic world events. Apart from small glimpses through war and conquest and other people's accounts, the people in Kyrgyzstan do not feature on the stage of world history. Instead, they live their lives in the fertile valleys sheltered by the Tien Shan mountains.

1

EARLY HISTORY

In order to understand the history of Kyrgyzstan, it would help to understand its geography. For much of its history, Kyrgyzstan was largely sheltered from the destructive events surrounding it.

Kyrgyzstan is a land of mountains, surrounded by some of the most majestic ranges of Central Asia. In the north and east, on its borders with Kazakhstan and China, runs the lofty Tien Shan mountain range. Within the Tien Shan stands Kyrgyzstan's highest mountain, the Victory Peak, towering at 24,406 feet (7,439 meters). In the south, bordered by both China and Tajikistan, are a number of ranges. These include the Kokshaal-Tau, Alay, and Atbashi. In the west, along Kyrgyzstan's border with Uzbekistan, is a smaller mountain range that surrounds the Fergana Valley.

The Alay, Gissar, and Tien Shan mountain ranges roughly enclose the Fergana Valley, which covers an area of more than 8,000 square miles (20,720 square kilometers). Well-irrigated by numerous rivers, the valley is marked by a stretch of fertile oases, though the lower reaches have salt marshes and sand dunes. The beauty and fertile land in this region, when compared to surrounding areas of Kyrgyzstan, have made the Fergana Valley one of the most densely populated areas of Central Asia.

Boundary representation not
necessarily authoritative

KAZAKHSTAN

N

⊛ Bishkek

Lake Issyk-Kul

VII

Toktogol
Reservoir

V

VI

IV

UZBEKISTAN

III

I

CHINA

II

TAJIKISTAN

AFGHANISTAN

| | International boundary |
| ⊛ | National capital |

I	Tien Shan
II	Alay Mountains
III	Fergana Valley
IV	Kyrgyz Range
V	Terskey Alataū Range
VI	Chatkal Range
VII	Fergana Range

0   50   100   150   Kilometers
0   50   100   150   Miles

The major mountain ranges of Kyrgyzstan can be seen in this topographic map drawn by the CIA. The major mountain range that runs through the country is the Tien Shan. Kyrgyzstan has been an isolated region for centuries as a result of its mountainous geography, although these same features have recently made the country a hot spot for tourists seeking dramatic views, natural landscapes, and mountain climbing.

Stelae, the Greek word for "pillars," are ancient stone slabs or tombstones, often carved to mark graves. Stelae have been found throughout the world and some date back as early as 900 BC. This stelae marks the grave of an ancient Kyrgyz warrior and was photographed in Kyrgyzstan in 1997.

While the Fergana Valley provides pleasant living conditions, historically it also made the outside world less accessible. The valley's population was isolated. Travelers and merchants considered the area an ordinary stop on the long journey to and from China and Arabia. Due to erratic borders drawn by the Soviets, much of the valley now falls in Uzbekistan, though parts are also in Kyrgyzstan and Tajikistan.

Kyrgyzstan boasts a few smaller fertile valleys, all in the north. One such valley is located near Mount Khan-Tengri, which contains Lake Issyk-Kul. The Chu and Talas river valleys are also fertile areas. The entire country is rich with many freshwater resources and crisscrossed by more than 30,000 rivers and streams. The current capital of Kyrgyzstan, Bishkek, is located in the Chu Valley.

Together, these hospitable lowlands make up only one-seventh of Kyrgyzstan's land mass, yet they are home to most of its population. The geography of Kyrgyzstan thus created conditions for isolated human settlements. People of neighboring settlements limited their interactions to hunting and gathering expeditions.

Early Settlements

Humans have been living in Central Asia for at least 100,000 years. Archaeologists have found evidence of human life in Kyrgyzstan dating back to the Stone Age. This evidence includes caves decorated with paintings and engravings of hunting scenes, as well as simple tools in the region around Lake Issyk-Kul and in the Chu Valley.

This is an aerial view of the meandering Syr-Darya River in Kazakstan, which originates in the Fergana Valley. The Syr-Darya is a long, winding waterway that flows 1,380 miles (2,220 km) through several Central Asian countries and into the Aral Sea in Uzbekistan. Too shallow to navigate by boat, the principle uses of the Syr-Darya are for crop irrigation and hydro-electric power.

The first inhabitants of Kyrgyzstan, like others in Central Asia, were nomads. These people moved back and forth across the region's vast grasslands in search of food. Asian nomads are believed to have been the first humans to tame horses and use them in their daily lives. Traveling on horseback enabled Asians to inhabit regions to the west as far as Turkey and Europe and to the east as far as Mongolia.

At the same time, people in other areas were making permanent or semipermanent settlements. Along the rich, fertile valleys around Lake Issyk-Kul and in the Fergana Valley on the banks of the Syr River, Asians were establishing villages. They were developing agriculture and irrigation systems.

This interaction between nomads and settlers helped Central Asia become more developed. Nomads roamed the steppe grasslands in search of pastures for their horses and occasionally raided settlements for food and supplies. Some settled down themselves, while others continued moving. This cycle of nomadic migrations continually brought new people and cultures into the oasis settlements.

Since these early nomads had not developed a script for their language, much of what we know about them is from accounts written by neighboring kingdoms. The first historical records of the Kyrgyz appear in Chinese chronicles dating around 2000 BC. These records refer to tribes in the west that were raiding and looting neighboring Chinese kingdoms. From these accounts, historians have reasoned that the Kyrgyz were nomads who originally lived around northwestern Mongolia. In the fourth and third centuries BC, Kyrgyz nomads raided Chinese settlements for food and goods. Unable to find any other solution, it is believed that the Chinese started building the Great Wall to protect themselves from these raids. In the following centuries, some Kyrgyz tribes had come under the rule of the Huns of Mongolia. After they escaped by moving into the regions of present-day Siberia, they spread into Kyrgyzstan's Chu and Talas Valleys around the sixth century AD.

The Scythians

In the meantime, by 800 BC, tribes known as the Scythians had also settled in Central Asia. The Scythians consisted of both nomadic and semi-settled tribes. Over time the Scythians moved northward, occupying the area around the Fergana Valley near the Syr River.

Ancient Greek historians have left behind accounts of Scythian settlements. Archaeologists have also discovered many burial sites rich with artifacts that provide information about these people. The Scythians were hunters and survived on fish and game. They also drank mare's milk. They loved gold and used it to make ornaments and to decorate household goods. Many gold offerings from this period have been found in royal burial mounds. The Scythians were famous for taming the horse and for skills such as archery and guerrilla warfare. They

Scythians are famous for their creativity and artistic craftsmanship, which is especially notable in their jewelry and other personal artifacts. This sixth-century BC gold belt buckle recreates a fight scene between a tiger and a wolf. Although the Scythians loved to work in gold, they also left behind artifacts rendered in a variety of other materials including wood, leather, bone, felt, silver, bronze, and iron. This piece is housed at the Hermitage in St. Petersburg, Russia.

frequently raided neighboring kingdoms to capture loot.

By the fifth century BC, inter-actions between three great civilizations—the Greeks, the Persians, and the Chinese—had led to the development of the Silk Road. The Silk Road was actually a number of trade routes that crisscrossed the present-day regions of Uzbekistan and Kyrgyzstan, connecting China, Persia, and Rome. These trade routes were called the Silk Road because the most prized commodity traded was silk from China, a product that no one else knew how to produce. The trade routes boosted local economy and contributed to the development of Sogdiana (the Fergana Valley) and surrounding regions as centers of government and culture.

The Scythians were first pushed north by the spreading Achaemenid Empire of Persia. In the fourth century BC, Alexander the Great, son of Philip II of Macedonia, set out in his

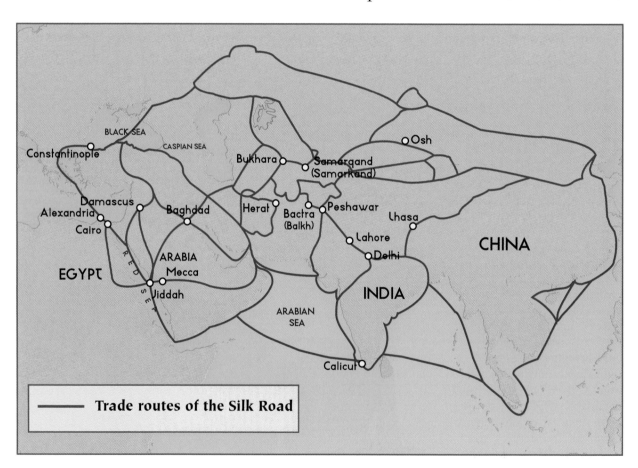

—— Trade routes of the Silk Road

The Silk Road was a series of routes over land and sea used during ancient and medieval periods. Traders and merchants used these routes to carry goods such as silk, wool, and precious metals from India and China, farther west through Central Asia, and on to the Mediterranean region. In addition to the sharing of goods, less tangible things were also "carried" along the Silk Road, such as religious ideas, works of litera-ture, inventions, and other cultural influences from distant lands.

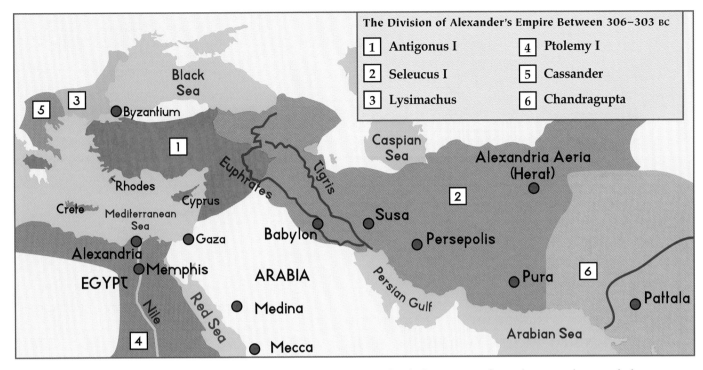

The Division of Alexander's Empire Between 306–303 BC

1. Antigonus I
2. Seleucus I
3. Lysimachus
4. Ptolemy I
5. Cassander
6. Chandragupta

After his death in 323 BC, Alexander the Great's empire was divided. Because Alexander's posthumously born son, Alexander IV, was too young to govern his father's vast territory, the younger Alexander spent his life as a figurehead without authority. Alexander the Great's vast empire was instead split among a number of people, a few of them former generals in his conquering army. This map shows the divisions of the empire between 306 and 303 BC.

conquest of the known world. After defeating the Persians, he pushed into Central Asia, driving the Scythian tribes north to Kyrgyzstan in 328–327 BC.

After Alexander conquered Transoxania and took Samarqand (present-day Samarkand, a city in Uzbekistan), he pushed the Scythians farther north. Alexander died in 323 BC, before he could consolidate his territories. After Alexander's death, his empire split into a number of provinces.

Over the next few centuries, the Hsiung-nu tribes, who were based in Mongolia, conquered most of Central Asia. A group of people within the Hsiung-nu tribes, the Yüeh-Chih (also known as Tokharians) created the Kushan Empire. This empire incorporated Kyrgyzstan and stretched all the way to northern India. The Kushans flourished on the wealth generated from the growing trade along the Silk Road between China and the Roman Empire.

2 THE KYRGYZ ARRIVE

The Kyrgyz did not always live in the region known as Kyrgyzstan. Historians believe that around the first century BC, they dwelled in the Yenisey River valley in central Siberia, now a part of Russia.

While some Kyrgyz settled in the Yenisey area, like other Turkish tribes, they were also migrating over the grasslands and the mountainous forest areas. Over time, the Kyrgyz faced hostile tribes from Mongolia, as well as from the Chinese Empire. For safety, they took security in the Chu Valley, near the foothills of the Tien Shan. These mountains provided a barrier from trouble in the north and west. This land, which was riddled with rivers, was known as Jetisu, Turkic for "Seven Rivers," or by its Russian translation, Semirechie. The natural pastures and grazing lands of this region were ideally suited to the Kyrgyz way of life, which revolved around the care of their animal herds.

CASPIAN SEA

Early settlements of Central Asian steppe farmers and shepherds can be seen on this map, which shows developments in the region between 2000 and 1000 BC. The various nomadic tribes of this period crafted wares in copper and bronze, used horses and wheeled vehicles for transport, and kept livestock principally for the purposes of obtaining milk to make cheese and yogurt. The nomadic nature of the tribes' livelihood in this region was due in part to climate changes and seasonal weather patterns that supported the vegetation grasses needed to feed animals. More permanent settlements began appearing in the region beginning in 450 BC.

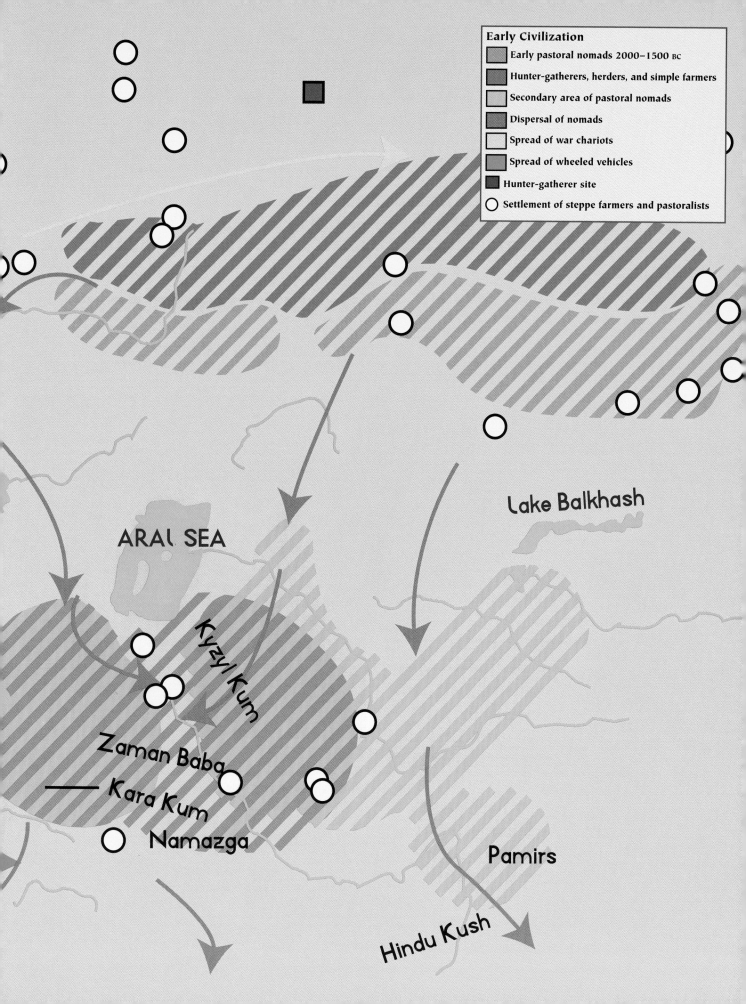

Early Civilization

Early pastoral nomads 2000–1500 BC

Hunter-gatherers, herders, and simple farmers

Secondary area of pastoral nomads

Dispersal of nomads

Spread of war chariots

Spread of wheeled vehicles

Hunter-gatherer site

○ Settlement of steppe farmers and pastoralists

Lake Balkhash

ARAL SEA

Kyzyl Kum

Zaman Baba

Kara Kum

Namazga

Pamirs

Hindu Kush

Daily Life

Medieval historical sources refer to the Kyrgyz as a light-skinned people with reddish hair and green eyes. This theory led modern historians to believe that the Kyrgyz were a part of the Turkic Tashtyk culture, a likely mix of Asian and European peoples.

The Kyrgyz were pastoral semi-nomads whose lives were built around the tending and breeding of their sheep and horses. They lived in gray-brown tents made of felt stretched over a flexible wooden structure that they called *boz ooyi*. The tents were round, generally twenty feet (six meters) in diameter, and had a smoke hole at the top. The Kyrgyz wore tall, white hats, also made of felt, which are still popular today. One proverb that has also survived illustrates the constantly moving and unstable nature of their daily lives: "The pasture is where you have tied your horse, your home is where you have made the fire."

The Kyrgyz were farmers and traders and exchanged goods such as furs and walrus ivory. They made earthenware pottery and household items out of wood and leather. One of the favored delicacies of the Kyrgyz to this day is fermented mare's milk, called *koumiss*.

Like other tribes of the region, the Kyrgyz practiced shamanism, a tribal belief system that had no official doctrines or scriptures. The central figure in this belief system was a shaman. The shaman was believed to have supernatural powers such as the ability to

This shamanistic shrine is one contemporary example of how similar shrines may have been constructed by early Kyrgyz tribes. Natural shrines were made of rocks and other objects. This one was photographed in Mongolia. Throughout the prehistoric world, shamanism was a common religion of people whose methods of survival were based around hunting and gathering food.

communicate with good and evil spirits and to use them to achieve certain outcomes. The most important goal was to ensure successful hunting expeditions. As more tribes came to adopt a more settled lifestyle concerned with livestock, the shaman's role evolved to meet these adaptations.

As the Turkic peoples spread over Central Asia, tribes began to develop defining specific characteristics. Their language also evolved into regional dialects. Over centuries, the Kyrgyz developed their own dialect, which helped in the evolution of their distinct identity. Although they are believed to have used a script, no written records of it have survived. There is one important historical work, however, that is believed to have originated at this time. Known as the great Epic of Manas, it was passed down orally from generation to generation until it was finally written down.

The Turkic Khanate

In AD 552, the various Turkic tribes organized under the leadership of the Kök Turks, forming a khanate. A khanate refers to a confederation of tribes governed by one overlord, or khan. The Kök Turk khanate was established by Bumin Khan. Chiefs of the individual tribes accepted his authority over matters of security and war. It was the khan's duty to assure that the tribes were safe from attacks. His other responsibilities included ensuring that the tribes had enough resources, usually accomplished by organizing raids to loot towns and cities, which were more developed and wealthier.

By 622, the empire of the Kök Turks stretched in a narrow strip from Mongolia to what are now Kyrgyzstan and Kazakhstan. The system had two centers of power, one in the Orkhon Valley of Mongolia with the "Eastern Turks," and the other in the Chu Valley with the "Western Turks." The Kyrgyz lived among the latter.

Bumin Khan died in 553, and his brother Istami took over the western wing. Bumin's son, Muqan, ruled in the east. The eastern wing faced constant military attacks from the neighboring Tang emperor, Tai-tsung, who reigned from 627 until his death in 649. The eastern wing had to accept the authority of the Chinese Empire from 630 to 680. Under Elterish Khan, who reigned from 683 to 692, the Kök khanate successfully resisted the Chinese and strengthened its hold on the Silk Road trade. The khanate finally ended in 744.

The Arabs

The Chinese Empire under the Tang dynasty had ambitions of conquering Central Asia, especially Transoxania and Sogdiana. They were, however, stopped in their tracks by the Arabs, a new power from the west.

In the seventh century, a new religion known as Islam had spread from Arabia through much of the Middle East. Followers of Islam, known as Muslims, formed armies that had defeated their strong, hostile neighbors, the Persians. By the eighth century, the Arabs had moved into

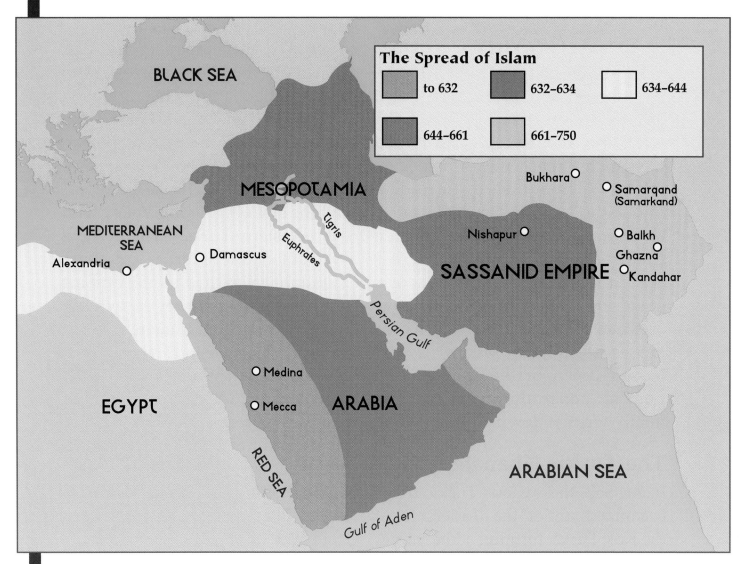

Arabs introduced Islam to the Kyrgyz tribes between the ninth and twelfth centuries, though the majority of Kyrgyz did not immediately convert. Mass exposure and conversion that later occurred during the seventeenth century is attributed to an invading force of Arabs known as Jungars. These Arabs drove the Kyrgyz out of the Tien Shan region and into the Fergana Valley where Islam was already established. Although many Kyrgyz reverted back to worshiping shamans after invading armies left the region, most of the Kyrgyz population had fully embraced Islam by the nineteenth century.

Central Asia. In 751, Arab armies defeated the Chinese on the banks of the Talas River, near present-day Jambul. Historians consider this battle a landmark since it ended Chinese ambitions. It also helped define a clear region of Central Asia outside of Chinese domination. Though some pockets of Turkish tribes remained within the Chinese sphere of influence, these were in Mongolia and the present-day Xinjiang province in China, often known as East Turkestan.

While the land of the Kyrgyz hosted this epic battle, the religion of Islam did not spread among them at the time. While those Kyrgyz who lived in the urban settlements were influenced by the religion and some even converted to Islam, the majority remained nomads living in the mountain forests who continued to practice shamanism.

After their victory, the Arabs, who were mostly an urban people, returned south and west to Transoxania, Samarqand (Samarkand), and Bukhara. Their interest in the mountainous regions was restricted to maintaining profitable trade routes; the Turkish tribes were free to do as they pleased.

Changing Hands

With the end of both the Kök khanate and the Tang dynasty, the

The Chinese emperor Hsüan Tsung (*second from left*) watches his favorite concubine in this Tang dynasty scroll, which was created during Tsung's reign between 712 and 756. In addition to his aspirations of conquering Central Asia, Tsung is remembered as a reform emperor of the Chinese Empire. During his reign he restored prosperity and stability to China, repaired its canal system, and waged several successful wars against the Turks, the Tibetans, and the Khitan. The Khitan eventually conquered sections of China in the ninth century and established the Liao dynasty.

Uighurs, a Turko-Mongolian people, established an independent kingdom in Mongolia. In 840, Kyrgyz tribes from the Semirechie and Yenisey defeated the Uighurs and drove them out of Mongolia, farther south into China. The Kyrgyz, however, did not move into central Mongolia. Since the Kyrgyz were content to exert control from the north, little trace remains of their rule. Within eighty years, they lost their hold on the region to a group known as the Khitans.

The Khitans, originally from northern Mongolia, conquered parts of China in the ninth century, establishing their own Liao dynasty. In 924, under their ruler, A-pao-chi, they defeated the Kyrgyz. A-pao-chi forced the Kyrgyz back to their old hunting grounds around the Tien Shan in the Semirechie.

The Khitans soon faced the turning tides of history and were defeated by the Juchen of Manchuria in 1124. Some Khitans fled westward, into the Semirechie and Chu Valley. Under Yeh-lü Ta-shih, they established the Karakhitai state centered in the city of Balasaghun.

The Karakhitai kingdom was even more short-lived. It had to accept the authority of the Qarakhanids, Turkish tribes closely related to the Uighurs, from the Semirechie and Kashgar in the Tarim basin. One of their khans, Satuq Bughra Khan, converted to Islam sometime in the

Cathay

In the medieval period, European travelers such as Marco Polo called China by the name Cathay. When European travelers and missionaries visited China in the eleventh and twelfth centuries, northern China was at the time ruled by a tribe known as the Khitans, or Khitai. To Europeans, it was only logical that the land of the Khitai be called by the similar sounding name Cathay.

The Venetian merchant Marco Polo is seen on horseback in this fifteenth-century French manuscript along with his father Nicolo and uncle Maffeo. Polo bids good-bye to the Mongol emperor Kublai Khan, grandson of Genghis Khan, who reigned between 1259 and 1294. Polo traveled from Europe to Asia in 1271 and remained there for seventeen years, during which time he served in the court of Kublai Khan. The account of his journey is known as *The Travels of Marco Polo*.

tenth century. His embrace of Islam led to a wholesale conversion of the Qarakhanid tribes. The Qarakhanids had already defeated the Samanids in Transoxania, taking Bukhara in 992, as well as Samarqand. The Qarakhanid lands were divided into provinces, with the main ruler residing in Balasaghun.

Plagued and weakened by rivalry within the ruling clan, the Qarakhanid tribes had to accept the authority of the emerging Seljuks. The petty chieftains existing under Seljuk rule were unsatisfied. The Karakhitais fought and defeated the Seljuks in 1141, ending their reign. This victory yielded little for the Karakhitai, or even the Khwarezm-shahs of Transoxania, who actually benefited from the defeat, since a stronger power was about to sweep through the region.

3 THE COMING OF THE MONGOLS

In the thirteenth century, a powerful and deadly force emerged from the northeast land once conquered by the Kyrgyz: the Mongols. This force destroyed and conquered everything in its path, inspired shock and awe among all it encountered, and created one of the largest empires ever seen in history. These were the great Mongols, a group of Turkic and Mongol tribes from Mongolia, led by the dynamic and ruthless Genghis Khan.

Genghis Khan

Genghis Khan, also called Chinggis, was born in Mongolia, probably in 1167. His father was a tribal chieftain related to the last khan of the Mongol kingdom. Named Temüjin at birth, Genghis Khan was orphaned in his youth and was unable to inherit his father's provinces. He

MEDITERRANEAN SEA

RED SEA

During the thirteenth century, the Middle East was overrun by hoards of Mongols, whose empire is seen on this map. Because they owned many horses, they excelled at horseback riding, especially in grouped formations. This extreme mobility and organization helped the Mongol Empire dominate new territories with little opposition. By the time of his death in 1227, Genghis Khan's territory extended from China to Persia (Iran). Three of his four sons, Jöchi, Chaghatai, and Ögödei, were his successors as well as a murderous bunch who also successfully expanded the empire until the fourteenth century.

EUROPE

Caspian Sea

Aral Sea

Karakorum
(Captial of Mongol
Empire after 1235)

Gobi Desert

MONGOLIA

Bukhara
(Bukhoro)

CHINA

Nishapur

Samarqand
(Samarkand)

KHWARAZMIAN
EMPIRE

Balkh

Bamian

Herat

ARABIAN SEA

Mongolian Empire

1227

1280

Route of Mongols in 1280

later formed an alliance with several other tribes. He took on the name Chinggis Khan, which some historians think meant "universal ruler."

Genghis embarked on a systematic conquest and unification of the other Mongol and Tartar tribes in Mongolia. His army consisted of skilled horseback archers, reportedly able to ride and sleep in the saddle for days at a stretch. They used this skill to achieve a deadly effect. By 1206, Genghis controlled all Mongol lands and called an assembly of tribal leaders at the river Onon, where he was named the khan of all Mongols.

The Mongol Storm

Genghis focused first on China, which had been a constant threat to Mongol power, and he captured Peking (Beijing) in 1215. Unable to conquer all of China, he moved westward, toward Transoxania. Genghis's conquest of the region had little effect on the Kyrgyz, who remained isolated in the forests.

When Mongol attention did turn to the Kyrgyz, they knew better than to resist. In 1207, they surrendered to Genghis's eldest son, Jöchi, and were left alone. By 1220, Genghis had taken over Bukhara, Samarqand, Tashkent (in present-day Uzbekistan), and Khojent (in present-day Tajikistan).

Genghis continued his conquests, bringing most of eastern Europe, Russia, Iran, the Caucasus, China, northern India, and Afghanistan under Mongol rule. Before his death in 1227, Genghis divided his empire into four *ulus* (segments). Eastern Europe, known as the Golden Horde, went to Genghis's son Jöchi; Transoxania and the rest of Central

Genghis Khan is seen in this miniature sixteenth-century Persian painting reading books with his four sons, Jöchi, Chaghatai, Ögödei, and Tolui. The painting is housed at the British Library in London, England.

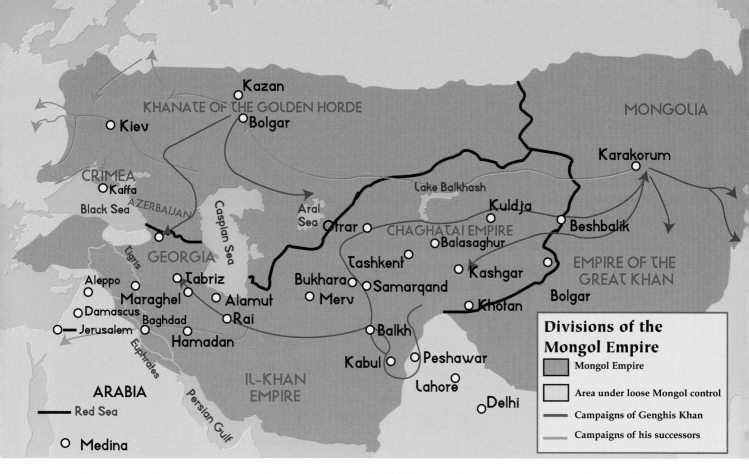

This map of the Mongol Empire shows its four main divisions and Mongol campaigns after the death of Genghis Khan in 1227. His blood successors, sons Jöchi, Chaghatai, and Ögödei, and grandson Kublai, ruled the empire during the thirteenth century and expanded the empire from present-day Beijing, China, to Istanbul, Turkey. Jöchi reigned over the Khanate of the Golden Horde; Chaghatai reigned over Transoxania and Central Asia; Mongolia and northern Russia was controlled by Ögödei; and China, or the Empire of the Great Khan, was ruled by Kublai Khan.

Asia went to another son, Chaghatai; the heartland of the empire, Mongolia and northeastern Russia, went to Ögödei; and China eventually went to his grandson Kublai (Qubilay). After the initial bloodshed, Mongol conquest created an era of relative peace and stability. Trade increased as merchants traveled from China all the way to Hungary, without fearing robbery or attacks or once stepping out of Mongol-controlled territories. The Mongols also developed the yam horse relays, an extremely fast communication system surpassed only in the nineteenth century.

The region of Semirechie and most of modern Kyrgyzstan fell under the ulus of Chaghatai and was known as the Chaghatai khanate. The Chaghatai khanate soon divided into a western and an eastern khanate. The western khanate consisted of Transoxania and most of modern Afghanistan, while the eastern khanate was composed of the land north of the Syr River, the Fergana

Valley, and the Semirechie, as well as present-day Kazakhstan.

The Chaghatai khans, who ruled from Bukhara, converted to Islam. The Chaghatai rulers realized the benefits of taxation and used this opportunity to increase their wealth through taxes and duties from traders, artisans, and craftsmen. This was in contrast to the eastern khanate, which became known as Mughulistan (in Arabic, "land of the Mongols"), where the people maintained the seminomadic traditions of their ancestors.

After the Mongol conquest and incorporation of the territory south of the Tien Shan, the area went through a period of deterioration. Under the Qarakhanids, it had experienced a development of urban centers, most notably Balasaghun in the Chu Valley. But the city was destroyed early on by the Mongols. As a result, the area slowly reverted to its pastoral origins. The land became grazing territory where the Mongols could maintain their centuries-old seminomadic lifestyle.

Burana Tower

Today, all that remains of the ancient city of Balasaghun is the Burana Tower, which was believed to have been built in the tenth century AD by the Qarakhanids. No one knows what its exact use was, but it seems to be the kind of minaret used for the Muslim call to prayer. It may have been part of a larger mosque complex. The Burana Tower has a narrow spiral staircase and is about 82 feet (25 m) tall. It originally had a height of 147 feet (45 m) and is the oldest minaret in Central Asia. It is about 62 miles (10 km) from the modern city of Tokmak.

The Burana Tower is one of the most widely known attractions in Kyrgyzstan and is visited by many tourists, historians, archaeologists, and Muslim clerics. Although earthquakes that occurred during the fifteenth century toppled its upper portion, the lower part of the tower is still clearly inscribed with information about daily life in tenth-century Kyrgyzstan.

Kyrgyz tribes that had remained in the Yenisey area now fell to the ulus of Jöchi, khan of the Golden Horde. As the Mongols gained power, more Kyrgyz joined the Mongol armies and moved westward with them. Historians believe that the biggest influx of Kyrgyz tribes into present-day Kyrgyzstan occurred from this time up to the sixteenth century.

Timur

During the last third of the fourteenth century, a Turkish-speaking

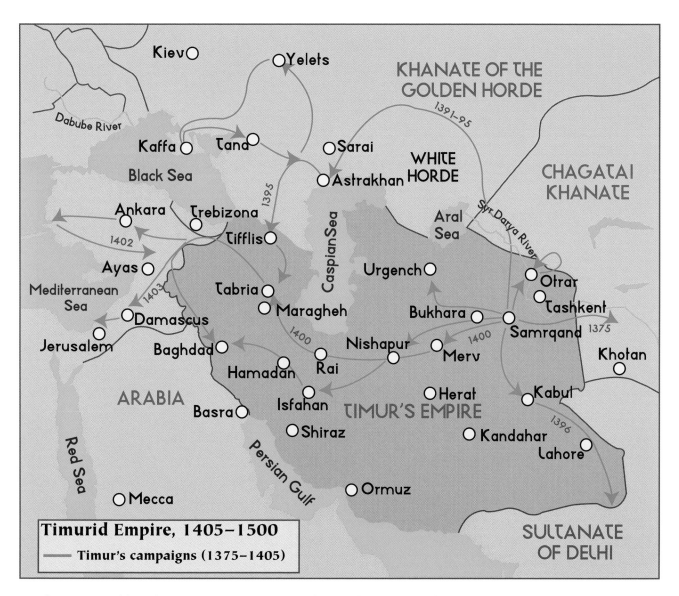

Timurid Empire, 1405–1500
— Timur's campaigns (1375–1405)

The expansive fifteenth-century Timurid Empire is illustrated in this map of Timur's campaigns and conquests. Timur, who claimed to be of direct Mongol descent, was one of Asia's most successful warriors after the great khans. His conquest of the region, which began as early as 1375, took nearly thirty years to complete. Timur is remembered most for leading campaigns where people were subdued by bloodshed, violence, and poverty. The Timurid Empire survived for approximately a century after Timur's death in 1405.

Mongol, Timur, whose name means "iron," gained control of the western Chaghatai khanate in Transoxania.

A skilled horseback archer and swordsman, Timur was born near Samarqand and grew to become chief of the Barlas tribe under the Chaghatais. Timur united the Turkish and Mongol tribes in Transoxania. He used them to expand his influence into Khorasan (Afghanistan), Khwarezm, Mughulistan, and Russia.

Along the way, Timur was injured and developed a limp, earning him the name Timur-lang (Timur the lame). Legend has it that he caught his attacker years later and used him for target practice.

After Timur conquered the western half of the Chaghatai khanate, the eastern segment enjoyed freedom. The Kyrgyz were able to overthrow their overlords in the Semirechie and Yenisey. But the independence was short-lived. By the following century, another confederation of tribes known as the Kalmyks conquered the region.

The body of the fourteenth-century conqueror Timur rests inside the Gur-e Amir Mausoleum in Samarqand, Uzbekistan. Although the mausoleum has weathered several earthquakes since it was constructed in 1405, it remains intact. The mausoleum's chapel is topped with a beautifully tiled dome, which is enclosed by a wall and archway. Its interior walls are inscribed in gold.

The Kalmyks were Mongols from the Tarim basin (Xinjiang province) and Mongolia, sworn enemies of the established Mongol Empire. In the seventeenth century, they began a century-long migration north, to their present home in southwestern Russia. They briefly controlled the regions in between, including southern Siberia and the Semirechie. The following centuries were also times of change, partly because the Manchu dynasty in China briefly exerted authority over parts of modern Kyrgyzstan.

The Uzbeks

In the fifteenth century, a group of Turko-Mongol tribes, formerly of the Golden Horde, had moved southward from the Ural Mountains. Known as Uzbeks, after their ancestor Oz Beg, a descendant of Genghis's son Jöchi, these tribes had migrated toward the Syr Darya by the mid-fifteenth century.

Under their leader, Abul Khayr Khan, the Uzbeks launched attacks on the Timurids and played an important role in local politics. Around that time, some of the tribes fled eastward, taking the name Kazakh, after which the state of Kazakhstan is named.

Muhammad Shaybani Khan, Abul Khayr's grandson, established the Shaybanid dynasty, which captured Bukhara in 1510 and formed two khanates, one based in Bukhara, and the other in Khiva (in Khwarezm).

By the late 1700s, Transoxania was divided among three Uzbek khanates, all claiming descent from Genghis Khan. These were the Qungrats, based in the city of Khiva in Khwarezm; the Mangits in Bukhara; and the Mings in Kokand (Quqon, Fergana), in the upper valley of the Syr Darya. In the early 1800s, the Kokand khanate annexed the territory of present-day Kyrgyzstan, building a fort in Bishkek to extend its control over the Chu Valley.

The Kokand khanate did have a favorable effect on its Kyrgyz subjects. The khanate established and developed the city of Bishkek, which is today Kyrgyzstan's capital. Education spread among southern tribes, and more Kyrgyz were exposed to Islam. The Kyrgyz were also able to occupy important positions in the khanate's administrative, military, and social structure.

4 | ENTER THE RUSSIANS

Perm

Simbirsk

Samara

Uralsk

ARAL SEA

Astrakhan

TURKMEN 1873

CASPIAN SEA

KHIVA

Over the centuries, Kyrgyzstan was continuously pulled under the influence of one or another of the lands of Central Asia and the Chinese and Mongolian territories. In the nineteenth century, yet another force, Russia, would flex its muscles in Kyrgyzstan's direction.

After the Uzbek conquest, the Kyrgyz yearned to be free. To this end, they sought help from other regional powers and sent ambassadors to the Chinese and the Russian Empires. After fighting and losing four wars against the Uzbeks between 1845 and 1873, the Kyrgyz renewed their efforts to gain outside support. At the same time, the constant rivalry between the different khanates, and their lack of a modern military and firearms, made the Kyrgyz more vulnerable to attack. This vulnerability fueled the possibility for foreign conquest.

During the sixteenth century, Russians advanced into Central Asia across Siberia from west to east. It was in those northern forest areas that nomads offered little resistance to imposing Russian hunters and traders. A dense animal population also provided Russians with a steady supply of animal pelts. Between 1816 and 1864, dominating Russian forces gained control over the Kazakhs. During the same period, Russians conquered the Caucasus region. Next, between 1865 and 1876, Russian forces dominated the former khanates of central Asia and became an imperial nineteenth-century empire.

Yekaterinberg

Tobolsk

Tyumen

Tomsk   Krasnoyarsk

Omsk
Aktyubinsk
1734–1822   Novo-Nikolayevsk

Akmolinsk
1731   Semipalatinsk

KAZAKHS   1881

1824

1854

Kazalinsk   1881

1853

Syr Darya

Vernyy

— Amu Darya

Tashkent

Samarqand

BUKHARA   TAJIKS

Ashkhabad

AFGHANISTAN   INDIA

Russia in Asia, 1815–1900

	Russian Empire, 1815
	Acquisitions 1816–1856
	Acquisitions 1856–1876
	Acquisitions 1700–1900
	Vassal Khanates
——	Railway

Russian Imperialism

Until the 1400s, many Russian territories had been under Mongol control. Timur's attacks on the Golden Horde weakened the Mongols. As a result, local Russian princes were able to free pockets of territory.

The first Russian intervention in Central Asia occurred in 1554. The Russian czar Ivan the Terrible conquered the Astrakhanid khanate, a Mongol kingdom on the Volga River. The khanate of Sibir (Siberia) was the next to fall, to Ivan's son, Fyodor.

With the rule of Czar Peter the Great, Russian interest in Central Asia grew. Peter realized the potential value of vast agricultural land that could provide the basis of economic growth in Russia. He was also driven by rumors of gold found in the Amu River in Transoxania. In this, he was copying other European powers like England, who had established colonies in Asia, Africa, and America to produce inexpensive agricultural raw materials like cotton, which were then processed into finished goods in factories and sold for a profit.

The Great Game

The eighteenth century saw the spread of British imperialism in Asia. Britain now controlled nearly all of India and was eyeing Iran and Afghanistan. The Russians soon grew worried that the British would also enter Central Asia and gain control of its vast grasslands, which would be ideal for agricultural plantations. The British, on the other hand, thought the Russians might advance through Afghanistan and attack India.

In what became known as the Great Game, both countries sent

Peter the Great (1672–1725), the founder of the Russian Empire, was czar of Russia from 1721 until his death. Peter helped industrialize Russia. He established modern cities, built a Russian naval fleet, and erected hospitals and schools. Peter the Great encouraged other reforms too, including simplifying Russia's alphabet, currency, and taxation system.

spies into each other's territories, trying to determine the conditions of Central Asia and what new steps would be taken. Traveling under the guise of hunting trips and scientific surveys, Russian and British spies returned with stories of exotic kingdoms and great wealth, spurring their respective governments to make the first move.

By the eighteenth century, the Kazakh hordes north of the Semirechie already had accepted Russian authority, and diplomatic relations had been established between the Russian capital, St. Petersburg, and the three khanates. Seeing that the rivalry between Bukhara and Kokand had left the latter weak, and encouraged by invitations from Kyrgyz rebels, the Russians moved south in 1853. In the next few years, they conquered the outlying territories of the Kokand khanate, including Kyrgyzstan, taking Bishkek, which they called Pishpek, in 1860. In 1863, at the request of the Bugu Kyrgyz tribe, the Russians built the fort of Aksu.

Worried by British advances, Russia annexed Tashkent and Samarqand in 1865. In the next few years it conquered Bukhara (1868), Khiva (1873), and Kokand (1876) but allowed them to exist as vassal khanates under Russian authority. Russia had become the fastest-growing imperial power, expanding at the rate of 86 miles (140 km) per day in the late nineteenth century.

In 1886, the Russians united all the khanates into a single province. They called this province Turkestan, with Tashkent as its capital. A Russian governor-general was appointed over Turkestan, but local khans were accustomed to collecting taxes on the czar's behalf.

Great Britain was alarmed at this consolidation, and it seemed as if the two powers were headed for a showdown in Afghanistan, a country that would bring Russia closer to the warm-water ports in what is now Pakistan. The two countries, however, were able to reach peace after an Anglo-Russian convention in 1907, effectively ending the Great Game.

Economic Conquest

Like other imperialist powers, Russia justified its conquests by saying that it was civilizing savages—another version of the "white man's burden" myth spun by the British. In reality, Russia now had access to what it called surplus land, which was actually territory that belonged to nomadic tribes. On this land, Russian farmers could grow cotton, a

Russian and British Empires, Turkestan, Mongolia, Tibet, and Neighbors

RUSSIAN EMPIRE

Tashkent

TURKESTAN

IRAN

Kabul

AFGHANISTAN

TIBET

PAKISTAN

BRITISH INDIA

NEPAL

Indian Ocean

This map shows the relationships between nations during the period of nineteenth-century Russian expansion. At the time, the Russian Empire was engaged with the British Empire in a competition for territory, a battle for supremacy over Central Asia known as the Great Game. Great Britain felt threatened by the speed of Russian expansion and feared that Russia would encroach upon the British Empire based in India. At the same time, Russia believed that Great Britain would expand its empire north throughout Central Asia since it had successfully maintained steady control over south Asia. The conflict between the two nations eventually focused on Afghanistan since the British believed that the Russians wanted to use the country to stage an invasion of British India. By 1907, the Great Game ended. The Russians accepted that Afghanistan was solely under British control, and the British agreed not to set their sights on Russian territories.

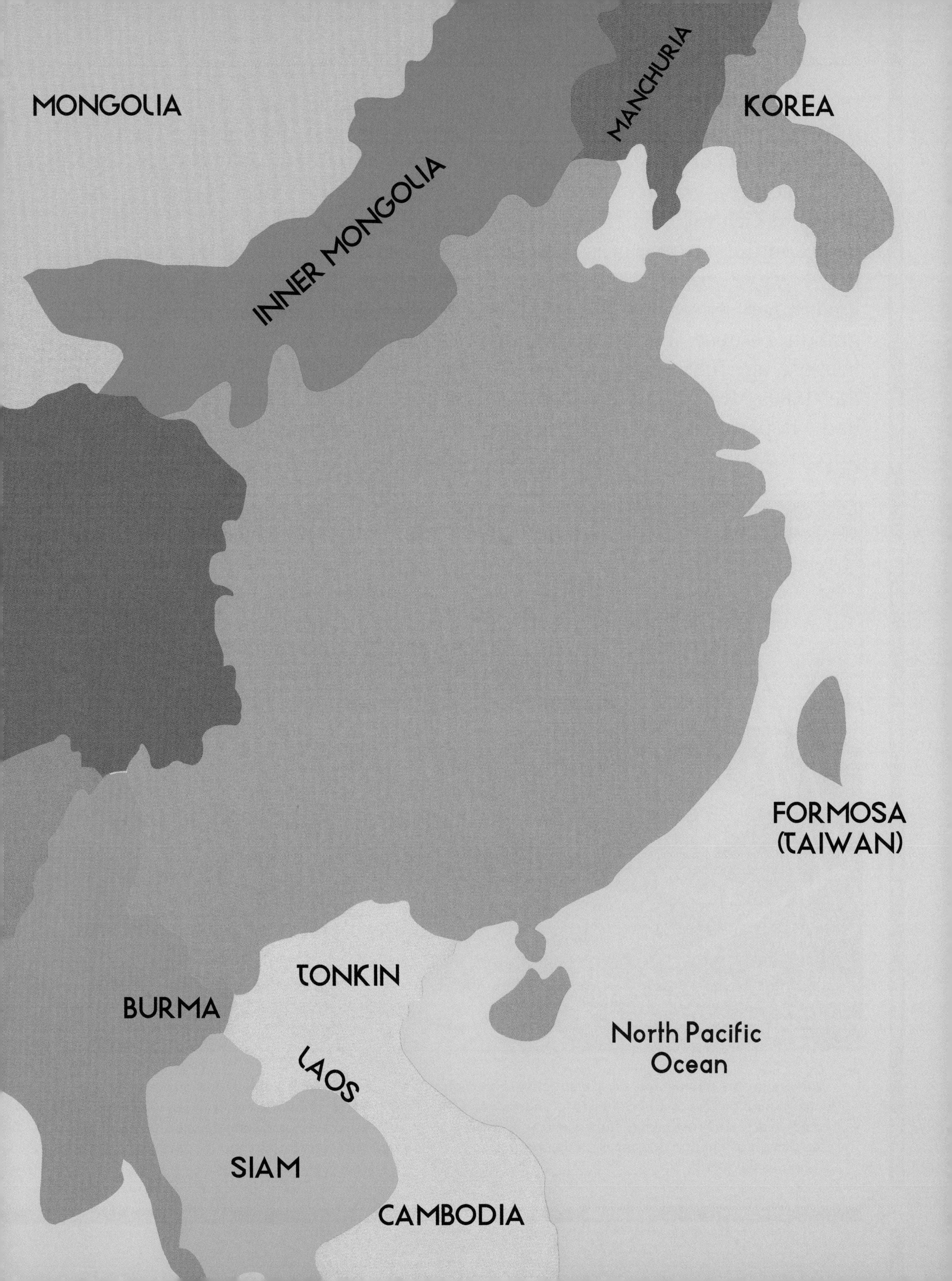

MONGOLIA

INNER MONGOLIA

MANCHURIA

KOREA

FORMOSA
(TAIWAN)

TONKIN

BURMA

LAOS

North Pacific
Ocean

SIAM

CAMBODIA

product in great demand in the international market.

Thousands of poor Russian peasants, escaping poverty and famine, fled into Central Asia. They set up farms on the pastoral grasslands of the Kyrgyz tribes. The Russian government encouraged this immigration because it had wanted to increase agricultural production. In the 1800s, Russian cloth factories had depended on raw cotton imported from America, but the American Civil War interrupted that supply. By the 1880s, using Central Asian land, Russia was growing enough cotton to meet its own needs and export more.

To facilitate the transportation of these goods and of people, the Russians built railroads, and by 1888, Samarqand, and later Tashkent, were linked in a network that connected the entire Russian Empire. The czar encouraged Russians to migrate to Central Asia, creating

Workers in this photograph are constructing a portion of the Trans-Siberian Railway in Russia, a major construction project that began in 1891 under Czar Alexander III. The continuous railway line, which was completed in 1904, stretches from Moscow to the port city of Vladivostok along the Pacific Coast. At a total length of about 6,000 miles (10,000 km) the Trans-Siberian Railway remains the longest single rail system in the world.

A bridge along the Trans-Siberian Railway is featured in this photograph taken during the time of its construction. Completion of this monumental transportation system helped industrialize and settle areas of the Russian Empire that had before been isolated. The line also helped bridge the vastness of the empire from "European" Russia to "Asian" Russia. All major Russian cities in the empire were linked in the vast rail system by 1916. Later, after World War II, the Trans-Siberian Railway joined the Trans-Manchurian Line, or the Ch'ang-ch'un Railway, in China.

enclaves of European settlements in major cities. In the first official census of Pishpek (Bishkek) in 1880, there were only six Kyrgyz in the whole town of more than 2,000 people. By 1914, there were 50,000 Russians in Bukhara alone.

This influx of foreigners had a disastrous effect on the Kyrgyz. Their seminomadic lifestyle as herdsmen was barely viable now, since all the pastures were being converted into Russian farms. Discontent grew day by day against Russian imperialism. Czarist rule also created confusion over names. The Russians had begun calling the Kazakhs, "Kyrgyz," to distinguish them from the "kazaky," the Russian term for Cossacks. Because they called the Kazakhs "Kyrgyz," they called the Kyrgyz "Kara-Kyrgyz."

The Jadidist Movement

Later in the nineteenth century, a new movement of young middle-class

Cossacks

Over various times in history the term "Cossack," which is derived from the Turkic *kazakh*, or "free man," has referred to different groups of Tartars and others in eastern Russia. It finally came to refer to the inhabitants of lands bordering the Caspian and Black Seas, who had a reputation as able fighting men. The Polish kings, and later the Russian czars, employed Cossacks in their wars, both invasive and defensive, and to crush rebellions. Because of this, the Cossacks acquired a notorious reputation, and the cry "The Cossacks are coming" induced great fear among eastern Europeans.

Russian officers in Petrograd watch the funeral of several Cossacks who were killed in September 1917 while defending the Russian government.

intellectuals from Turkestan emerged that challenged Russian imperialism. Called the Jadidists, these Turkish activists believed that all aspects of Central Asian society, especially religion, had to be united and reformed in order to overthrow the Russians. The movement promoted modern education and was marked by a pride in the various peoples and their Turkish heritage, and it promoted pan-Turkish nationalism, making "Unity in language, thought, and action" its slogan.

The Jadidists were unsuccessful in their attempt to win independence. However, one of their goals, the overthrow of the Russian Empire, was achieved by another movement, the Socialist revolution.

5 KIRGHIZ SOVIET SOCIALIST REPUBLIC

At the turn of the twentieth century, the Russian Empire was marked by great political and economic turmoil. While the elite classes, especially the aristocrats and feudal lords, led rich luxurious lives, peasants and artisans starved in the countryside. In this environment, Marxism, a new political and economic philosophy found followers in Russia.

Marxism

The theory of Marxism evolved from the writing of Karl Marx in the late 1800s. Karl Marx was a philosopher who was appalled by the economic conditions in his native Germany and his new home, London. He saw that the Industrial Revolution and the subsequent factories were creating wealth and prosperity, but the workers who toiled in the factories did not benefit from their own labor. Factory owners and businessmen were growing wealthier by selling products made by the workers for great profits, but workers themselves were paid very low wages.

Marx felt the basic root of this problem was private property, which made people corrupt and greedy. In modern industrial society, with its mass production, there was no excuse for poverty or hunger. His solution was a revolution. He felt that workers should

German-born revolutionist, historian, and writer Karl Heinrich Marx (1818–1883) was dedicated to advancing the idea that capitalist political systems should be overthrown and replaced with Socialist/ Communist systems. His most acclaimed writings include *The Communist Manifesto* (1848), which he wrote with Friedrich Engels, and *Das Kapital* (1867)

rebel and overthrow the capitalist system and instead establish a Socialist system, in which the state owns everything. Socialism would create the condition for the last phase, Communism, in which everyone owns everything. Each person would work, and each would receive wages and compensation in keeping with their needs. "From each according to his ability, to each according to his need," was a common phrase attributed to Marx.

After Marx's death, people inspired by his writings applied these theories to specific conditions in which they lived, leading to modified versions, including Russian, or Soviet, Marxism.

Russian Revolution

The Marxist movement grew in strength and popularity in the early 1900s. The czarist regime and its cruel exploitation of workers and peasants disgusted Russian intellectuals. They believed the czar should be overthrown through a revolution of the people. Led by Vladimir

Areas of Russia where peasants led uprisings during the First Russian Revolution of 1905 are indicated on this map. Freed peasants, even though they could now own property, were angered that they were allowed to purchase far less land than they originally farmed under the older system. Other farmers were forced off their land to work in Russia's factories. Major rebellions took place in St. Petersburg ("Bloody Sunday") and in Odessa, supported by the crew of the battleship *Potemkin*. These and other uprisings led to the formation of the Duma, or elected assembly, of the Russian Parliament.

St. Petersburg

Baltic Sea

Dvinsk ○ *Dvina River*

○ Moscow

RUSSIAN EMPIRE

Lodz

Dombrovo

○ Kiev

Dnieper River

Volga River

Dniester River

Don River

Odessa ○

Black Sea

The First Russian Revolution, 1905–1907

Peasant unrest and land seizures

TURKEY

Members of the Bolshevik Red Cavalry are seen in this 1919 photograph. The Red Army, which grew to more than 500,000 members under Leon Trotsky, was originally a militia of Bolshevik volunteers. This photograph was taken one year before the army defeated Russia's czarist government during the Russian civil war, which led to the formation of the USSR.

I. Lenin, the Russian Marxists, who were called Bolsheviks, attempted to seize power in 1906 but failed. Their second attempt in 1917, with their own Red Army, was successful. The Bolsheviks set up "soviets" or councils, in cities and provinces, to take over the local governments. Members of the CCCP, the Soviet Communist Party, now manned the government.

The Jadidists supported the Bolshevik Revolution because the Soviet Marxists had always criticized the czar's imperialist policies and his colonies in Central Asia. They had promised that if they came to power, they would free the colonies and let them choose if they wanted to be part of their Marxist experiment or instead become totally independent.

In 1916, there was a huge Jadidist rebellion, in which the Kyrgyz played a major role. The rebellion helped weaken the czarist administration. After the revolution, the Jadidists thought they would be liberated. They even established an independent government in Kokand in 1918. But their illusions were shattered. The Tashkent soviet, or council, dispatched troops to crush the Jadidists, who continued to fight for freedom. Eventually, the Bolsheviks dominated, and they incorporated Turkestan into the Soviet Union.

Soviet Republics

The Soviet government in Moscow soon realized that it would be easier to control Turkestan through a "divide and rule" policy. One by one, it redrew the boundaries, carving out "autonomous republics." These were Uzbek, Turkmen, Tadzik, Kazakh, and Kirghizia (present-day Kyrgyzstan) from 1917 to 1924.

Kirghizia was declared a Soviet Socialist republic in 1936, and a strip of land from the Fergana Valley,

including the cities of Osh and Jalalabad, was added to it. Pishpek was made the capital of Kirghizia, and the name was changed to Frunze, in honor of a Communist hero, M. V. Frunze, and finally to Bishkek.

Each state had its own government, similar to that in Moscow, but in spite of the title "republic," they were not free. Moscow appointed the government leaders and controlled the policies. In this way, it was able to weaken the ideology of Turkic nationalism. Soviet officials made it a point to exaggerate the difference among the various Turkic peoples. Common histories, languages, traditions, and populations of the area were divided among local "nationalities." Historians have called this weakening and distortion of a culture's heritage ethno-engineering. It is a process that redraws boundaries and rewrites history to change people's perception of their ethnic identity.

Another way of weakening Turkic nationalism was to eliminate local culture and language by compulsory "Russification." Central Asian people were forced to study Russian in order to obtain jobs, and the script of their Turkic languages was changed from Arabic to Latin, and later to Cyrillic (Russian). Russians were encouraged to migrate to the republics so that the Turkic peoples would become a minority in their own land. By 1959, the percentage of Kyrgyz in Kirghizia had fallen to 40 percent from 66 percent.

At the same time, the Soviets tried to erase religion from all of Russian society, including Central Asia, by banning all religious activities. This meant that the Kyrgyz, who were Muslims, could not practice Islam, and they couldn't go to mosques, make pilgrimages to Mecca, or learn Arabic. They were even forbidden from owning a copy of the Koran. In 1917, Turkestan had 25,000 mosques. By 1942, that number had decreased to 1,700. Faced with the impossibility of ever fully achieving its goal, the Soviet government decided that it would be easier to control religion than to completely suppress it. It instead established government committees to regulate religious affairs and appointed heads of mosques.

Leaders in Moscow controlled economic policies. The biggest problem was that the Kirghizia economy was never developed in a self-sufficient manner. Instead of a healthy mix of agriculture, industrial production, and a services sector, the Soviets used the republic for whatever they needed. They decided to use the Kyrgyz for their

M. V. Frunze

Mikhail Vasilyevich Frunze (1885–1925) was born in Pishpek. At a young age, he got involved with the Bolsheviks and became a commander in their Red Army. Frunze played a major role in the fall of the Kremlin and the later wars the Soviets fought to keep the Russian Empire from falling apart. Frunze also helped stop rebellions in Turkestan, defeating the Jadidists, whom the Soviets called Basmachi. He became the *commissar*, or secretary for war, and enforced conscription, or a mandatory military draft. After Lenin's death, many of his close colleagues, including Frunze, were killed or died under mysterious circumstances.

Mikhail Vasilyevich Frunze, seen in this undated photograph, is best remembered for taking part in the October Revolution of 1917 and for his role as commissar for the Russian army and navy between 1924 and 1925.

traditional skills as herdsmen, placing emphasis on raising sheep for high-quality wool. The authorities forced local herdsmen to increase their number of herds, placing a growing burden on the region's pastures and water resources. At the same time, the republic was mined for gold and mercury, depleting its natural resources. Thus Kirghizia was dependent on Moscow and other republics for technology, manufactured goods, and other services.

In 1967, the people of Frunze rebelled. Although a police beating of a drunken soldier sparked the initial uprising, it quickly turned into an anti-government protest. Rioters attacked the local police and KGB offices. The KGB was the Soviet Union's secret service. The Soviet army soon put down the rebellion.

In the 1980s and 1990s, after seventy years of Socialism, it was clear that the Soviet Union's policies were failing. Across the country, people were unhappy with Communist Party rule, and they wanted a more open, responsive government. They began to express their discontent aggressively, and their protests marked the beginning of the end for the USSR.

6 INDEPENDENCE

In 1985, the Soviet president, Mikhail Gorbachev, decided to respond to demands for a change in Soviet government. He introduced reforms known as *glasnost* (openness) and *perestroika* (political and economic reform). Although he believed that these reforms would strengthen the government, they instead led to the collapse of the Soviet Communist system.

With glasnost and perestroika, people increased their protests against Communism. The central government in Moscow became unstable, with Gorbachev stuck between pro-democracy protesters and Communist Party members who believed he was a "soft" leader. The situation erupted further when the radical dissenters attempted a coup to depose Gorbachev. The republics, now alarmed at this attempted overthrow, declared themselves and

Independent Kyrgyzstan is seen in this contemporary map. Since the collapse of the Soviet Union in 1991, Kyrgyzstan, with its predominately agricultural economy, has had difficulty making the transition from a Communist to a democratic nation. Former Soviet president Mikhail Gorbachev (*inset*) served the Soviet Union as leader from 1985 until 1991 and is credited with helping to end the Cold War between the Soviet Union and the United States.

KAZAKHSTAN

Stepnoy
BISHKEK
Kara-Balta

Lake Issyk-Kul
Karakol

Toktogul

Kochkor

Naryn

At-Bashy

Jalal-Abad

CHINA

Kara-Darya

Osh

Sary-Tash

Comparative Soviet Nationalities by Republic

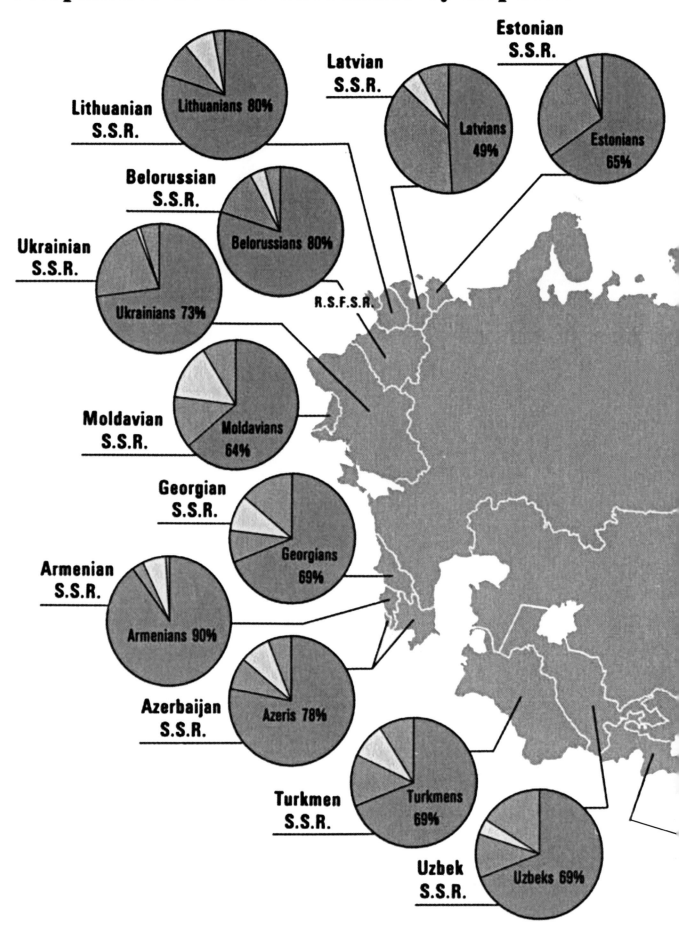

Lithuanian S.S.R. — Lithuanians 80%

Latvian S.S.R. — Latvians 49%

Estonian S.S.R. — Estonians 65%

Belorussian S.S.R. — Belorussians 80%

Ukrainian S.S.R. — Ukrainians 73%

R.S.F.S.R.

Moldavian S.S.R. — Moldavians 64%

Georgian S.S.R. — Georgians 69%

Armenian S.S.R. — Armenians 90%

Azerbaijan S.S.R. — Azeris 78%

Turkmen S.S.R. — Turkmens 69%

Uzbek S.S.R. — Uzbeks 69%

Republic	Titular Republic Nationality	Russian	Minor Nationality	Other
R.S.F.S.R.	–	84%	Ukrainians 4%	12%
Ukraine	Ukrainians 73%	21%	Jews 1%	5%
Belorussia	Belorussians 80%	12%	Poles 4%	4%
Estonia	Estonians 65%	28%	Ukrainians 3%	4%
Latvia	Latvians 49%	38%	Belorussian 5%	8%
Lithuania	Lithuanians 80%	9%	Poles 8%	3%
Moldavia	Moldavians 64%	13%	Ukrainians 14%	9%
Georgia	Georgians 69%	8%	Armenians 9%	14%
Armenia	Armenians 90%	3%	Azeris 6%	1%
Azerbaijan	Azeris 78%	8%	Armenians 8%	6%
Uzbek	Uzbeks 69%	11%	Tajiks 4%	16%
Kazakh	Kazakhs 40%	40%	Ukrainians 6%	14%
Tajik	Tajiks 59%	11%	Uzbeks 23%	7%
Turkmen	Turkmens 69%	13%	Uzbeks 9%	9%
Kirghiz	Kirghiz 48%	28%	Uzbeks 12%	14%

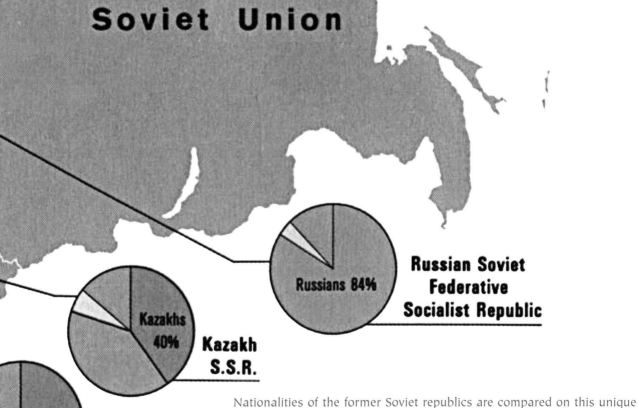

Soviet Union

Russians 84%

Russian Soviet Federative Socialist Republic

Kazakhs 40%

Kazakh S.S.R.

Kirghiz 48%

Kirghiz S.S.R.

Tajiks 59%

Tajik S.S.R.

Nationalities of the former Soviet republics are compared on this unique map. Since 1991, Kyrgyzstan has faced increased tension between certain ethnic groups, especially between the Kyrgyz and Uzbek communities. This conflict stemmed from discrimination by native speakers of the Kyrgyz language and those who speak only Russian. The tension has caused many Russians to leave Kyrgyzstan. As a result, the country's economy has faced a slow recovery since many of the Russians were skilled workers. In 2001, President Akayev helped solve this problem by making Russian an official language of Kyrgyzstan.

their respective legislatures independent of Communist policies.

In this climate of unrest, a lower-level Communist Party member became president of Kirghizia for the first time. His name was Askar Akayev. Akayev, a scientist, was nominated by the parliament after the regular presidential candidates failed to secure a majority. The parliament also renamed the republic Kyrgyzstan. Communists, however, continued to have much influence in Kyrgyzstan, and they attempted to overthrow Akayev in a coup. Akayev survived the attempted overthrow and got the parliament to vote for separation from the Soviet Union in 1991.

Political Change

The Soviet system was not a democratic system. While there were elections, they were meaningless because there was only one party. The Communist Party controlled everything. Communist Party members filled every position in the government and administration.

After independence, however, there were high hopes that Kyrgyzstan would become a true functional democracy, with a multiparty system and free elections. The new president, Akayev, promised to overhaul the political system and introduce democratic reforms. Akayev became the first president of the independent state after winning elections in October 1991. He retained his power through elections held in both 1995 and 2000. The first elections were believed to have been fair, but in 1995, local opposition leaders alleged that they were rigged, and in 2000, even outside observers were shocked, saying the elections were unfair and staged.

While there is a multiparty system in Kyrgyzstan, in reality, the government harasses opposition parties and makes it difficult for them to function, especially to contest the elections in any meaningful way. At the same time, Akayev has moved to increase his own powers by limiting those of the legislature and judiciary. There are no effective checks and balances, since the president can overrule other branches of government.

Kyrgyzstan's president Askar Akayev casts a ballot during the presidential election in Bishkek on October 29, 2000. Although the six other competing candidates claimed the election was undemocratic and contested Akayev's victory, it marked his third term in office. Opposition leaders were once barred from running because they failed a difficult Kyrgyz language test.

Economic Decline

Independence had severe economic consequences for the new state. Kyrgyzstan now has limited natural resources and is the second poorest country in Central Asia. According to some estimates, one-third of its

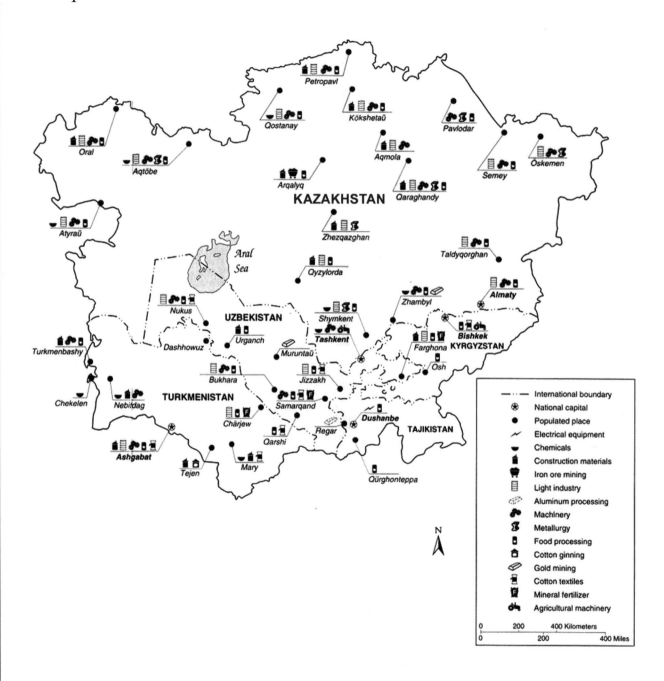

Legend:

- – · – International boundary
- ⊛ National capital
- ● Populated place
- Electrical equipment
- Chemicals
- Construction materials
- Iron ore mining
- Light industry
- Aluminum processing
- Machinery
- Metallurgy
- Food processing
- Cotton ginning
- Gold mining
- Cotton textiles
- Mineral fertilizer
- Agricultural machinery

| 0 | 200 | 400 Kilometers |
| 0 | 200 | 400 Miles |

The major industries of Central Asia are illustrated on this map compiled by the CIA. Kyrgyzstan's industrial exports include gold, mercury, uranium, natural gas, and electricity. The country's main agricultural exports are cotton, tobacco, wool, and meat. Despite Kyrgyzstan's slow economic growth, its leaders are hard at work implementing strategies to reduce poverty and encourage greater foreign investments in the country.

population now lives below the poverty line, meaning that they are unable to afford basic necessities of life such as food and shelter.

Under the Soviets, the republic had never been allowed to develop a strong economy. It had been dependent on the central economy for many goods, technology, and aid. With the collapse of the Soviet Union, the republic lost this support. The few industries that remained experienced serious declines in production, as they lost their main market and most people did not have sufficient purchasing power.

Under the Soviet regime, everything was owned by the state. After independence, Akayev attempted to privatize the economy by letting private businessmen take over companies. This process, however, has been slow. Many businesses are still run by the government, which is accused of corruption and inefficiency. Many state-run enterprises

Jamal Marayeva orders her children to wash their hands after playing near their felt-covered *yurt* (portable tent) near Cholpon-Ata, Kyrgyzstan, in October 2000. Many Kyrgyz still live in yurts and migrate from season to season. They say that they feel too disillusioned by poverty to take part in the democratic process of electing leaders by voting.

even fail to pay their employees. A black economy, in which people sell goods illegally without paying taxes, has flourished, causing more losses to the state in terms of revenue. The government also faces a high budget deficit and huge foreign loans. Another problem the country has faced is the number of Russians leaving the republic, leading to a shortage of skilled workers, technicians, and scientists.

Agriculture is the one sector that has seen some improvements in Kyrgyzstan. Its main crops are wheat, barley, maize, potatoes, and melons. Some regions also produce cotton and tobacco.

Social Unrest

As we have seen, the Soviets drew the borders of Kirghizia in an arbitrary manner, and the new state of Kyrgyzstan inherited problems

This elderly Kyrgyz farm worker places tobacco leaves on lines to dry naturally in Uzgen, Kyrgyzstan. Since the former collective state-owned farms known as *kolkhoz* have been privatized in Kyrgyzstan, tobacco has become one of the country's greatest cash crops. At least 300,000 Kyrgyz currently work in the tobacco industry, which includes two American companies.

Kyrgyz soldiers guard their headquarters in Batken, the most modern area of a mountainous and desolate area of Kyrgyzstan. More than 750 radicals, members of Uzbekistan's Muslim opposition movement, descended on Batken in 1999, occupying villages and holding hostages. The radicals stationed themselves in the region for several weeks after crossing the Kyrgyzstan border from Tajikistan and displaced about 5,000 Kyrgyz in the process.

associated with its new borders. There is a large concentration of Uzbeks in the Osh region in the Fergana Valley. The Fergana Valley itself is another cause of conflict, since two of Kyrgyzstan's neighboring countries, Uzbekistan and Tajikistan, also share parts of that fertile territory. All three nations believe that the valley should belong only in their country. Land is the key issue, especially since Kyrgyzstan has fewer regions conducive to settlements and agriculture, and the valley is rich and fertile. Even before independence, rioting broke out between Uzbeks in Osh and local Kyrgyz as a result of the Soviet-drawn divisions. In 1999, Uzbek militants seized several towns near the border with Tajikistan, which was racked by civil war at the time, and in 2000, the Kyrgyzstan army fought Uzbek guerrillas based in Tajikistan who had infiltrated into the Fergana Valley.

Another problem is the social development and modernization of Kyrgyz society. Much of Kyrgyzstan is still rural, and its social structure remains based on tribal and ethnic relationships. These groups place constant demands on the government, putting immense pressure on the regime, which is hard-pressed to please them while implementing reforms in the political system. At the same time, Akayev made the mistake of appointing local leaders, thus encouraging a family and clan-based network of nepotism, patronage, and corruption.

What Lies Ahead

Akayev came to power talking about democracy and reform. But during his years of rule, the government in Kyrgyzstan has evolved into an authoritarian regime similar to the Soviet system but without the Marxism. It has never enjoyed a fully functional democracy. Kyrgyzstan's next election is scheduled for 2005.

The developments in Afghanistan after the September 11, 2001, terrorist attacks in the United States have had a negative effect throughout the region, including in Kyrgyzstan. With the U.S. bombing and subsequent occupation, the region became unstable. The current government in Afghanistan has not been able to take control of the whole country and pockets of warlords and militants still exist. Militants from Afghanistan are believed to have moved into neighboring Uzbekistan and Tajikistan, leading to fears of increased militancy in the region. Kyrgyzstan had already been facing problems in the Fergana Valley from Uzbeki militants, who operate out of Kyrgyz and Tajik territory.

The economy is still unstable, and young Kyrgyz have few opportunities to improve their standard of living. This poverty can lead to further social unrest in the country and can provide ideal recruitment conditions for an angry citizenry eager to join militant organizations.

Afghans, pictured living in a refugee camp in the village of Khwaja-Bahauddin, are provided with food from Russia and the Central Asian republics, including Kyrgyzstan. Kyrgyz workers aided the Afghans in 2001 during the U.S.-led war in Afghanistan and provided about 300 trucks filled with nearly 9,000 tons of food as part of the United Nation's World Food Program.

TIMELINE

2000 BC Kyrgyz tribes attack outlying regions of Chinese Empire.

800 BC Scythian tribes inhabit region of present-day Kyrgyzstan.

328 BC Alexander the Great invades Central Asia.

AD 552 Kök Turk khanate unites Turkic tribes, including Kyrgyz, under one ruler.

600 Kyrgyz people migrate south from the Yenisey River region into Semirechie region.

751 Arab army defeats the Chinese in Battle of Talas, in Kyrgyzstan.

840 Kyrgyz tribes defeat the Uighurs, driving them into Mongolia.

924 The Khitans defeat the Kyrgyz, driving them back into Semirechie.

999 The Qarakhanids take control over region, establishing a capital, Balasaghun.

1141 The Karakhitai defeat the Seljuk Turks near Samarkand.

1167 Genghis Khan is born in Mongolia.

1207 Kyrgyz tribes surrender to Genghis's son Jöchi.

1227 Genghis Khan dies; Kyrgyzstan falls under domain of his son Chaghatai.

1364 Timur defeats the Chaghatai khans, establishing himself as emir (ruler).

1400 Uzbek tribes move into the region of modern-day Uzbekistan and Kyrgyzstan.

1510 Shaybanid dynasty conquers Bukhara, establishing khanates in Bukhara and Khiva.

1554 Russian czar Peter the Great conquers the Astrakhanid kingdom.

1700 Central Asia divided between three Uzbek khanates: Kokand, Khiva, and Bukhara.

1800 Kyrgyz comes under the rule of the Kokand khanate; Kyrgyz rebel but are defeated.

1876 Russians conquer the khanate of Kokand and bring Kyrgyzstan into their empire.

1891 Construction of the Trans-Siberian Railway begins.

1905 First Russian Revolution.

1917 October Revolution in Russia; Communists suppress Turkish nationalists (Jadidists).

1921 Kyrgyz regions become part of the Turkestan Autonomous Soviet Socialist Republic.

1924 Soviets form the Kara-Kirgiz Autonomous Region (Kirghiz Autonomous Region).

1926 Kirghiz Autonomous Region upgraded to Soviet Socialist republic.

1936 Kyrgyzstan becomes a constituent republic within the USSR.

1990 Askar Akayev, a liberal within the Kyrgyz Communist Party, is elected president.

1991 Kirghiz republic changes name to Kyrgyzstan and declares independence.

1993 Kyrgyz legislature approves first independent constitution.

1994 Voters approve constitutional amendment to make the legislature a bicameral (legislature based on two chambers, such as the House and the Senate) body.

1995 Kyrgyzstan holds its first elections; Akayev is reelected by a majority.

1996 Referendum approves constitutional amendment that concentrates more power in the hands of the president while limiting the powers of the legislature; Uzbek militants seize towns in Kyrgyzstan near Tajikstan.

2000 Akayev is reelected president for another five years.

2003 Referendum approves constitutional reforms and expands the power of the presidency.

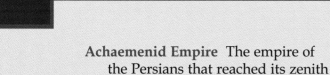

GLOSSARY

Achaemenid Empire The empire of the Persians that reached its zenith under Cyrus the Great in 559 BC.

Bishkek The present-day capital of Kyrgyzstan.

Bolshevik A member of the extremist wing of the Russian Social Democratic Party, which seized power in Russia during the revolution of November 1917.

Central Asia A region composed of Kazakhstan, Kyrgyzstan, Tajikistan, Turkmenistan, and Uzbekistan; located south of Russia, west of China, and east of Iran.

cold war A conflict of ideological differences carried on without full military action, and usually without breaking up diplomatic relationships. A condition of rivalry and mistrust between countries.

Communism A political and economic system based on Marxism in which all property is shared.

coup (coup d'état) A French term meaning "blow to the state," referring to a sudden, unexpected overthrow of a government by outsiders.

Cyrillic The script in which Russian is written.

czar A ruler of Russia until the 1917 revolution.

divide and rule A political strategy of dividing the citizenry of a country in order to dominate that country. The philosophy behind this strategy is the belief that a country can be easily weakened if its citizens are not unified

enclave A distinct unit enclosed within a foreign territory.

imperialism The policy or practice by a nation to exert power over another country's territory and/or to gain control over that country and its resources indirectly, often to the point of exploitation.

Marxism The political, social, and economic principles advocated by Karl Marx, especially a practice of Socialism that led to the development of Communism.

Mongolia A region of east Asia that includes the Gobi Desert.

nationalism Loyalty and devotion to a nation, placing an emphasis on the promotion of its culture and interests above others.

nepotism Favoritism.

Persian One of the major language families spoken in Central Asia, which includes Pashto and Tajik.

shamanism A religion that was practiced by the indigenous people of far northern Europe and Siberia.

Silk Road A series of travel routes that caravans took through Central Asia linking China and India to western Europe.

Turkic People of Turkish ethnicity; one of the major language families spoken in Central Asia, which includes Kazak, Kyrgyz, Turkmen, and Uzbek.

Union of Soviet Socialist Republics (USSR) The Soviet Union, which existed between 1922 and 1991 and was composed of territory between eastern Europe and northern Asia bordering on the Arctic and Pacific Oceans and the Baltic and Black Seas.

white man's burden The alleged duty of white people to manage the affairs of the less-developed nonwhite people.

FOR MORE INFORMATION

Asia Society and Museum
725 Park Avenue at 70th Street
New York, NY 10021
(212) 288-6400
Web site: http://www.asiasociety.org

Association for Asian Studies
1021 East Huron Street
Ann Arbor, MI 48104
(734) 665-2490
e-mail: jwilson@aasianst.org
Web site: http://www.aasianst.org

Central Eurasia Project
The Open Society Institute
400 West 59th Street
New York, NY 10019
e-mail: jburke@eurasianet.org
Web site: http://www.eurasianet.org

Silk Road Foundation
P.O. Box 2275
Saratoga CA 95070
e-mail: info@silk-road.com
Web site: http://www.
      silk-road.com/toc/index.html

Web Sites

Due to the changing nature of
Internet links, the Rosen Publishing
Group, Inc., has developed an
online list of Web sites related to the
subject of this book. This site is
updated regularly. Please use this
link to access the list:

http://www.rosenlinks.com/liha/kyrg

FOR FURTHER READING

Anderson, John. *Kyrgyzstan: Central
    Asia's Island of Democracy?* New
    York: Routledge, 1999.
Frye, Richard N. *The Heritage of
    Central Asia from Antiquity to
    the Turkish Expansion*. Princeton,
    NJ: Markus Weiner
    Publishers, 1996.

MacLeod, Calum. *Uzbekistan: The
    Golden Road to Samarkand*. New
    York: McGraw Hill/Contemporary
    Books, 1997.
Stewart, Rowan. *Kyrgyzstan* (Odyssey
    Illustrated Guides). New York:
    Odyssey Publications/W.W.
    Norton Company, Inc., 2002.

BIBLIOGRAPHY

Dari, A. H., et al., eds. *History of
    Civilizations of Central Asia.*
    Volumes I–IV. Paris: UNESCO
    Publishing, 1994.
Encyclopaedia Britannica. "Central
    Asia, History of." Retrieved March
    2, 2002 (http://www.brittanica.
    com/eb/article?eu=114577>).
Encyclopaedia Britannica. "Kyrgyzstan,
    History of." Retrieved February 12,
    2003 (http://www.brittanica.com/
    eb/article?eu=114579).

Erturk, Korkut A. *Rethinking Central
    Asia: Non-Eurocentric Studies in
    History, Social Structure and
    Identity*. Reading, UK: Ithaca
    Press/Garnett Publishing, 1999.
Hunter, Shireen T. *Central Asia Since
    Independence*. The Washington
    Papers. Westport, CT: Praeger
    Publishers, 1996
Soucek, Svat. *A History of Inner Asia*.
    Cambridge, UK: Cambridge
    University Press, 2000.

INDEX

About the Author

Aisha Khan is a journalist from India now based in Los Angeles. She has always had a fascination for Central Asia and Afghanistan—the former being the subject of her master's thesis at New York University and the latter, the home of her ancestors.

Photo Credits

Cover (foreground), pp. 1 (map), 4–5, 48–49 © 2002 Geoatlas; cover (background), p. 1 (background) © Library of Congress, Geography and Map Division; cover (top left) © Janet Wishnetsky/Corbis; cover (bottom right), pp. 53, 57 © Reuters New Media Inc./Corbis; cover (top right), pp. 11, 28 © Daniel Samuel Robbins/Corbis; pp. 6–7, 10, 50–51, 54 courtesy of the General Libraries, the University of Texas at Austin; p. 8 © Corbis; p. 12 © Yann Arthus-Bertrand/Corbis; pp. 13, 22, 34, 38, 39, 42, 44, 46 © AKG Images; pp. 14, 15, 16–17, 20, 24–25, 27, 29, 32–33, 36–37, 43 maps designed by Tahara Hasan; p. 18 © Adrian Arbib/Corbis; p. 21 © The Art Archive/Freer Gallery of Art/The Art Archive; p. 26 © The Art Archive/British Library; p. 30 © Charles and Josette Lenars/Corbis; p. 40 © Underwood and Underwood/Corbis; p. 49 (inset) © Peter Turnley/Corbis; pp. 55, 58 © AP/Wide World Photos; p. 56 © Janet Wishnetsky/Corbis.

Design: Tahara Hasan; **Editor:** Joann Jovinelly;
Photo Researcher: Elizabeth Loving